thirtyONE days

Rediscovering Your Identity

Bill McClure

WestBow
PRESS
A DIVISION OF THOMAS NELSON

WestBow Press books may be ordered through booksellers or by contacting:

WestBow Press
A Division of Thomas Nelson
1663 Liberty Drive
Bloomington, IN 47403
www.westbowpress.com
1-(866) 928-1240

ISBN: 978-1-4497-4828-9 (hc)
ISBN: 978-1-4497-4797-8 (sc)
ISBN: 978-1-4497-4798-5 (e)

Library of Congress Control Number: 2012906489

Printed in the United States of America

WestBow Press rev. date: 4/12/2012

This book is dedicated to my Father, the Great I AM; my Lord and Savior, Jesus Christ; and my spirit's best friend, the Holy Spirit. I am nothing without You.

INTRODUCTION

Before we jump in, I feel the need to let you know a bit of my history. Many people that really know me would be shocked to hear about me writing a book. I went through high school and college (undergraduate and graduate levels) without ever writing more than a ten page paper. Writing was just something that didn't come naturally. That began to change in 2010 at a conference in Camp Hill, Pennsylvania. The Voice of the Prophets (VOP) conference was hosted by Global Awakening and featured many speakers including Graham Cooke, Larry Randolph, Jamie Galloway and others. At this conference, I was given a prophetic word that was recorded and put on a website for me to download. When I returned home, I listened to that word over and over again. I even typed it all out and I still carry copies of it in my wallet and Bible. In the spring and summer of 2010, I read through my prophetic word and was encouraged that God had me where He wanted me to be. The word talked a lot about being a teacher and writing curriculum and enjoying children. I am currently a teacher in a middle school so this is very accurate! At that point in my life, that was all I got out of it, but I was encouraged!

In October of 2010, I attended the Voice of the Apostles (VOA) conference in Baltimore, Maryland (also hosted by Global Awakening). At this conference, I began to step out of my comfort zone and ask God about where I was headed. I was happy about the previous prophetic word that reassured me of my current placement in the world, but I wanted to know where He was leading me. Unfortunately, the answer didn't come at the conference. I was quite upset. A few months later, my mom attended a small meeting that was being led by Jamie Galloway. At that meeting, Jamie prophesied over her and at one point told her that God was going to clear her son's head and answer the question that was on his mind. This got me exited! God was talking about me through others! So I waited, and waited, and waited.

Eventually, I got frustrated with waiting and complained to my wife that nothing was happening. Her response was exactly what I needed. She told me to go back and reread my prophetic word from VOP 2010. As I read it, I saw things in the words that I never noticed before. One line really triggered something in me. It said, "I see the Lord saying that he is giving you ideas, so start writing, you write a lot, but start writing, start putting it down." I had been reluctantly asking God for a few weeks if I was supposed to write and I never received what I would call a "clear" answer; however, now that I look back I can see how it was so obvious. So I began writing, I wrote down a lot of random things, but every time I started, situations popped up that got me sidetracked. Finally, a home church that my family was attending began a teaching night that came around once a month. As soon as they mentioned this, I began to think about topics that I would enjoy teaching. The first topic I thought of was that we as Christians need to really understand who we are. I created a PowerPoint on everything I could think of that related to this topic and was quite relieved when I finished. I even prayed and asked God if more information was needed and no new information came, so I felt that it was complete. I e-mailed the completed work on to the home church leader and the others that were leading the teaching time. Then over the next few weeks I started interjecting some of these thoughts into our church discussions. They were not received very well. Many people were upset or confused by my comments. I quickly understood that I would not be able to teach this lesson anytime soon. So, why did God have me create this PowerPoint? Why did I spend so much time researching and praying for answers?

The answer instantly came; I was supposed to be writing about this topic. God told me that the writing that He was talking about in that prophetic word, was a book dedicated to reminding Christians who they are in Christ. I began typing and typing and typing. I looked at my page count and it climbed higher and higher (remember I've never written something longer than ten pages). I know that God was working because I knew that I could not write this much! About half way through writing, I began to wonder how I was going to get this edited and published. I worried for months about this and even stopped writing, because doubt crept in. In October of 2011, I attended the VOA 2011 conference in Lancaster, Pennsylvania. I went with my wife and three small kids. I went with that gnawing worry in the back of my brain that just kept creeping up and telling me that I would never get this done, and that no one would edit it or publish it. During one session, I was talking with a man that had been sitting by us for a few sessions. He was telling me about how God had been impacting him at the conference. Then he asked me if God had been talking to me also. I told him my story and he was very understanding. In fact, his wife was in the same position. She is in the middle of writing a book and is worrying about editing and publishing! It was comforting to know that I was not alone. He gave me the same good advice that he had also given his wife: "If God has told you to write this, and He wants others to know what you wrote, He will make sure it gets to them!" That one comment released my worry and encouraged me to give the problems of this book over to Him and allow Him to work it all out. This is that book, and if you are reading it, it is because God really wanted it to get into your hands!!

Day 1

"God is love"

1 John 4:16

As we start this study, I think we need to begin with who God is. After all, a major component of who we are in Christ is to know who God is. God is far more than the Great Spirit or the "Big Man Upstairs." He is everything!

God is love! Now that may sound corny or the good Christian-way to define God, but it is true. God is love because God created love! Love is *impossible* without God. In fact, without knowing God, you cannot love! That is quite sad for the unbelievers that think they can, but if God is love and they do not know God, how can they love? Humanity was created to love our Creator and His creation. Our very existence demonstrates how much he loves us.

Another example of His love is that we have free will. Love cannot exist in a "slave/owner" relationship. Love cannot be forced upon someone. It can only exist when those involved have an option NOT to love!

1 John 4 is full of truths about God's love and how we love in return.

> "Dear friends, let us love one another, for *love comes from God*. Everyone who loves has been born of God and knows God. Whoever does not love does not know God, because God is love. This is how God showed his love among us: He sent his one and only Son into the world that we might live through him. *This is love: not that we loved God, but that he loved us and sent his Son as an atoning sacrifice for our sins*. Dear friends, since God so loved us, *we also ought to love one another*. No one has ever seen God; but *if we love one another, God lives in us and his love is made complete in us*." 1 John 4:7-12 (italics added)

Isn't it amazing to consider that the Creator of the Universe loved us from the formation of the world! God loves us so much that He mapped out our lineage from generations past to make sure that we were born exactly when we were needed to impact the situations of the world! God is amazing!

It is also great to know that if we love, God lives in us AND His love is made complete in us! We are the tools that cause His love to become complete. It is not enough for Him to love us; we must accept that love and pass it on to one another. When that happens His love is completed!

CONSIDER:

- How has God shown His love for you in the last week?

  _____

  _____

  _____

  _____

- How does He usually show His love for you?

  _____

  _____

  _____

  _____

- How have you shown your love for God in the last week?

  _____

  _____

  _____

  _____

- How do you usually show your love for Him?

  _____

  _____

  _____

  _____

- Who have you loved to make God's love complete?

  _____

  _____

  _____

  _____

ACTION:

- Today, make it your mission to show your love to everyone you come into contact with (spouse, children, boss, co-workers, teachers, parents, siblings, strangers).

_____

_____

_____

_____

_____

_____

_____

_____

_____

_____

_____

_____

_____

_____

_____

_____

_____

_____

_____

_____

_____

_____

_____

_____

_____

_____

_____

_____

_____

Day 2

"And He will be called Wonderful Counselor, Mighty God, Everlasting Father, Prince of Peace."

Isaiah 9:6

"No one is good—except God alone."

Mark 10:18

God is more than just love, he is also peace. All peace comes from Him! In fact, Isaiah calls Jesus the "Prince of Peace". We have probably heard that many times and have allowed it to simply run out of our mouths without thinking much of it, but if we really think of the words; we realize that He is the Royal Son to the King of Peace. If Jesus is the Prince, God is King!

Peace also needs to be defined. Peace is not the absence of something. Many people see peace as the absence of war or conflict, but peace is a state of mutual harmony. Having peace means that you are in a good mood, and living in harmony with everything around you.

With this definition, we can understand God's title much easier. God is the King of Peace. He is the ruler of everything that is good and right. He is *always* in a good mood. He is *always* good.

It is at this point that most people can understand the words, but do not display those feelings in their life. For example, many of us will agree that God is good all the time, but if a hurricane, tornado, famine, or other natural disaster hits a nation we tend to believe that God sent the storm. We also seem to think that God causes people to become sick. Nothing can be further from the truth. God does not cause calamities! He is good all the time, and saying that he causes disasters and illnesses says that He can do things that are not good.

What most people do not see is that God knows everything! He can look into the future and see the end result. He sees Satan bringing a problem your way and He is thankful for it, because He knows how you are going to come out of it! He knows that what Satan intended for evil, we have the ability to turn around for God's glory.

The best example of this is Job. Job had it all, he was rich, had an amazing family, and a great relationship with God. Satan went into the throne room of God and God began bragging about how great Job was. Satan's solution was to attack Job and his family so Job would denounce God. God looked into the future, saw what was going to happen and allowed Satan to play his game. Satan killed off all of Job's children, took away all of his wealth and caused him to be sick to the point that Job's own wife told him to "curse God and die," but Job remained faithful! Eventually Satan had to admit that nothing could keep Job away from God and he withdrew his attacks. Now if we ended the story there it would be an amazing testament to the persistence and loyalty of a man to God, but it continues. Because of Job's faithfulness, God gave everything back to him . . . EVERYTHING! In fact, God gave Job MORE than what he had in the beginning. God knows how to bless those that are true to him!

CONSIDER:

- How has God shown his goodness to you?

  _____

  _____

  _____

  _____

- How have you shown God's goodness to others?

  _____

  _____

  _____

  _____

- Think of something that is close to your heart (maybe your family, job, or talent), would you still love God if it were taken away from you?

  _____

  _____

  _____

  _____

- When bad things happen, do you blame God, or laugh at Satan because what he intended for evil will be used to glorify God?

  _____

  _____

  _____

  _____

ACTION:

- If problems come your way today, laugh in Satan's face and look for God's blessing!

_____

_____

_____

_____

_____

_____

_____

_____

_____

_____

_____

_____

_____

_____

_____

_____

_____

_____

_____

_____

_____

_____

_____

_____

_____

_____

_____

Day 3

"See what great love the Father has lavished on us, that we should be called children of God!"

1 John 3:1

Throughout the Bible God is referred to as a Father. This perception is traditional and goes back to the beginning of time. From the Creation, God was referred to as Father.

In reality, God is a Spirit and does not have a gender. He is neither male nor female. If this is true, then why has He always referred to Himself as a Father?

In order to answer this, we need to understand that God has the ability to do anything! He can look into the future and know exactly what is going to happen in detail that we cannot even comprehend. Knowing this, I believe that at Creation, God looked into the future and saw that what the world lacked was not Mothers, but rather, Fathers. This world that we live in is full of children that grow up without a father. Some lose their father to illness and death, while others lose fathers through divorce or abandonment. Some children even lose their fathers due to a workaholic attitude. Some children even grow up not knowing who their father actually is. It is sad, but unfortunately, a common occurrence in today's culture.

God knew this situation before he created light on the first day. He determined that what the world needed from Him was not a genderless God, but one that represented perfection in fatherhood. Now we can look to a perfect Father in Heaven!

God's fatherly appearance in the Bible is a major contributor to how people react to the family atmosphere in churches today. After all, a church is made up of believers that are all brothers and sisters of Jesus! With God as our Father figure and Jesus as our brother, we should spend every minute together as if we were one big family because we are!

CONSIDER:

- How has God displayed himself to you? Has it come in a fatherly role or some other type?

  _____
  _____
  _____
  _____

- How have you shown God's fatherly appearance to others?

  _____
  _____
  _____
  _____

- In what ways has God supplemented the "father-figure" in your life?

  _____
  _____
  _____
  _____

ACTION:

- Thank God for His fatherly role in your life. Thank him for the truth that we are to be called his son or daughter.

_____

_____

_____

_____

_____

_____

_____

_____

_____

_____

_____

_____

_____

_____

_____

_____

_____

_____

_____

_____

_____

_____

_____

_____

_____

_____

_____

Day 4

"For since the creation of the world
God's invisible qualities—his eternal power
and divine nature—have been clearly seen,
being understood from what has been
made, so that people
are without excuse."

Romans 1:20

Over the last three days, we have looked at some of the characteristics of God. If the intent of this devotional was to describe every aspect of God's character, we could be here a *long* time. However, the Bible helps us out a bit and says that God's qualities are clearly displayed all around us through what He has made. He did this so that there is no excuse for not knowing Him.

Many people have asked the question about what happens after death and the answer of Heaven and Hell are generally accepted, but come with several questions. The main problem that people have with this idea is that there are people that will die and go to Hell and never have a missionary visit them and give them the choice to hear the gospel. Romans 1:20 answers that question. When we are born, we have a hole in our lives that only God can fill. When we look at God's creation, we feel a sense of awe and beauty that points us to the One that created it. When we recognize the Creator, that hole in our lives becomes filled. Creation proclaims the glory of God. If there is no one around to preach the message of the kingdom, even the rocks will cry out and tell of what Jesus has done for us. There is no way that God would allow someone to die without the opportunity for them to receive His son as the payment for their sinfulness.

A great example of this is "Abraham's Bosom." Luke 16 tells the story of the beggar named Lazarus and the rich man. Lazarus lay at his gate and was covered with sores, while the rich man had everything he could ever ask for. When they both died, Lazarus was escorted by angels into Abraham's Bosom and the rich man into Hades. Lazarus' life afforded him the opportunity to stay in Abraham's Bosom until Jesus made the need for such a place obsolete. Abraham's Bosom was created as a place for the righteous to go until Jesus had done his redemptive work on the cross.

Matthew 12:40 (ASV) says, "For as Jonah was three days and three nights in the belly of the whale; so shall the Son of man be three days and three nights in the heart of the earth." When Jesus died, he went into Abraham's Bosom (the heart of the earth) to tell the righteous that had died from Adam to John the Baptist about what He came to earth to do. Those in Abraham's Bosom had the ability to accept Jesus or reject Him (as a side note, the thief on the cross next to Jesus was the first man to die under the New Covenant and therefore was the first to go directly into Heaven!).

Now if God had thousands of years worth of righteous people in Abraham's Bosom waiting for Jesus to come and save humanity from the punishment that they deserved, I think he could use His creation to preach his message of salvation to remote villages across the world. After all . . . He has done it before (Numbers 22:21-34).

CONSIDER:

- We have discussed three aspects of God's character, what are some others that are important to you?

_____

_____

_____

_____

- What is something in God's creation that proclaims His glory?

_____

_____

_____

_____

ACTION:

- Make a list of several remote areas around the world that need to hear the gospel message. Pray for each nation or city so that even if missionaries cannot get to the remotest areas, the rocks will cry out and proclaim the goodness of the Lord.

_____

_____

_____

_____

_____

_____

_____

_____

_____

_____

_____

_____

_____

_____

- Preach the gospel to all of creation (Mark 16:15).

_____

_____

_____

_____

_____

_____

_____

_____

_____

_____

_____

_____

Day 5

"In your majesty ride forth victoriously in the cause of truth, humility and justice; let your right hand achieve awesome deeds."

Psalm 45:4

It is inevitable that, when we begin talking about who we really are, others will begin to think we are being prideful. Pride is a major issue today, especially in the church! Many people in the church will take every chance they get to discredit their own abilities. They have a "woe is me" attitude and will generally put themselves down at every turn. This is actually an odd form of pride. Pride has nothing to do with how great you are; instead it has everything to do with how much you talk about yourself! True humility is not thinking less of yourself, but rather thinking of yourself less. So when we delve into your greatness, realize that admitting that you have awesome attributes is not a form of pride, but rather truth.

Imagine that you painted a portrait of someone and we are together admiring your work of art. If I say, "This painting is awful, look at the colors! This painting is worthless; someone just needs to take it out of my sight," would this be honoring to you as the painter? Of course not! In the same way, God created you. For you or someone else to say how wretched you are and how messed up your life is dishonors the one that created you! To recognize that God doesn't make mistakes and that you are exactly who you were created to be is honoring to Him!

Along with this is yet another concept I want to clear up before we begin discovering who you are. Many people define their lives by things that make no real difference in this world. Many people allow their jobs or career to define who they are and this is the beginning of becoming a workaholic. Others are defined by their roles in the family, accomplishments, or even their financial portfolio. Allowing external things to define your life is a form of idol worship. You are placing these definitions of your life ahead of who God says you are! Ultimately, God's view of who you are is all that matters.

CONSIDER:

- What are some things you say about yourself that may come across to others as being prideful?

  _____

  _____

  _____

  _____

- When you say these things do you believe you are being prideful?

  _____

  _____

  _____

  _____

- How do you define your life? Are you a mom, dad, brother, sister, CEO, teacher, mechanic, winner of a certain award, rich or poor? Do these classifications define your life?

  _____

  _____

  _____

  _____

ACTION:

- Take one day and do not say anything negative about yourself.

_____

_____

_____

_____

_____

_____

_____

_____

_____

_____

_____

_____

_____

_____

_____

_____

_____

_____

_____

_____

_____

_____

_____

_____

_____

_____

_____

_____

_____

Day 6

"So in Christ Jesus you are all children of God through faith, for all of you who were baptized into Christ have clothed yourselves with Christ."

Galatians 3:26-27

Let's get started on describing who we are. First of all, we are children of God. In order to identify who we are, we need to build up from our foundation. Our connection with God is the strongest foundation we have. God created each and every one of us. He knows us better than we know ourselves. He knew us and loved us before we were born. In fact, Jeremiah 1:5 says, "Before I formed you in the womb I knew you, before you were born I set you apart!" What an amazing thought! The Creator of everything created us the way we are and calls us His children. We all have physical parents, but God is the One that *really* created us. You are a son or daughter of the One that created everything on the planet.

The Bible says a lot about being called children of God. Here are a few examples:

- Matthew 5:9—Blessed are the peacemakers, for they will be called children of God.
- Romans 8:14—For those who are led by the Spirit of God are the children of God.
- Romans 8:16—The Spirit himself testifies with our spirit that we are God's children.

The most amazing verse, however, is Romans 8:19 which says, "For the creation waits in eager expectation for the children of God to be revealed." This verse is so powerful to think about. God's creation is waiting for us to be revealed. It's waiting for us to take our rightful place among creation! I have heard it said that "water is longing to be walked on again." Again, this is amazing. Water, which is a part of creation, has had so many amazing experiences throughout the earth's existence. Massive amounts of it have been parted in the Red Sea and Jordan River, Jesus and Peter have walked on water, and Jesus turned water into wine! It is an awesome concept to know that water, and the rest of creation, longs to see God's children revealed!

CONSIDER:

- List some of the benefits of being God's child.

  _____
  _____
  _____
  _____

- If we acknowledge that we are God's children, then it follows that God is our Father. This is a good thought, but many people minimize God down to how their own physical fathers acted. For example if your physical father was distant, you may view God as distant, or if your father was a harsh disciplinarian, then God must be the same. How do you view God?

  _____
  _____
  _____
  _____

ACTION:

- Make a list of as many characteristics of God as you can. Reflect on how these characteristics help shape you view of God as your Father or you as God's child.

_____

_____

_____

_____

_____

_____

_____

_____

_____

_____

_____

_____

_____

_____

_____

_____

_____

_____

_____

_____

_____

_____

_____

_____

_____

_____

_____

_____

_____

_____

Day 7

"For I have betrothed you to one husband, that I may present you as a chaste virgin to Christ."

2 Corinthians 11:2 (NKJV)

The term "Bride of Christ" does not exist in the Bible. However there are verses like 2 Corinthians 11:2 that make it obvious that we are to be his bride.

So what does this mean for us? We are going to become married to Jesus one day. At this point in time we are "engaged" and he is in Heaven preparing a place for us.

> "I am going there to prepare a place for you. And if I go and prepare a place for you, I will come back and take you to be with me that you also may be where I am." John 14:2-3

This is very fun to research because this is also what happens in the traditional Jewish weddings! After a man and woman were engaged, the bridegroom and his father would return home to prepare a place for the couple to live in. The couple would not see each other for several months while the home was being built. Now many people in this situation would assume that the future groom would build quickly to get to his wedding day as fast as possible. However the groom was not the one that decided when he could return for the bride, it was his father that determined the time and place for the grooms return.

This should all sound very familiar. Jesus is in Heaven with God preparing a place for us. Jesus cannot wait for us to be reunited with him in Heaven, but God the Father is the only One that knows the time and place for His Son to return to the earth for His bride.

> "But about that day or hour no one knows, not even the angels in heaven, nor the Son, but only the Father." Matthew 24:36

So what do we do as one who is engaged to the Son of God? We make ourselves ready for His return! Jesus is returning for a spotless virgin, one who is perfect in every way! Make yourself ready!

> "Let us rejoice and be glad and give him glory! For the wedding of the Lamb has come, and his bride has made herself ready." Revelation 19:7

CONSIDER:

- What have you done in the last week that has proven your love for Jesus?

  _____

  _____

  _____

  _____

- How has Jesus shown his love for you in the last week?

  _____

  _____

  _____

  _____

ACTION:

- Research the traditional Jewish wedding and notice the similarities between it and the returning of Christ for his bride.

_____

_____

_____

_____

_____

_____

_____

_____

_____

_____

_____

_____

_____

_____

_____

_____

_____

_____

_____

_____

_____

_____

_____

_____

_____

_____

_____

_____

_____

_____

Day 8

"Now the one who has fashioned us for
this very purpose is God, who has given us
the Spirit as a deposit, guaranteeing
what is to come."

2 Corinthians 5:5

This may sound cliché, but we were created for a purpose. Every person that has ever been born and every person that will ever be born has a role to play in this life. Your purpose defines who you are!

Before your birth God saw that there was going to be a problem. That problem may have been anything from a disaster to God wanting another person to love. He knew exactly what the problem was and created something to fix it. The thing He created was you! You were created in your mother's womb to solve a problem that God foresaw. Your purpose in this life is to fulfill that mission!

Too many people claim that God cannot use "Little Ol' Me," but that simply is not true. God created you to be useful. He created you with a plan in His mind! You are powerful because the Creator lives inside of you! When you become saved, you are no longer permitted to say that you are "merely human." You are FAR more than that! You are a body that has your own spirit and the Holy Spirit co-existing inside. What an amazing thought!

Ephesians 1:11-12 says "In him we were also chosen, *having been predestined according to the plan of him who works out everything in conformity with the purpose of his will,* in order that we, who were the first to put our hope in Christ, might be for the praise of his glory." We were chosen according to the plan of God! He chose US! We were not the pursuers . . . we were pursued! God made you and knows everything about you. He knows more about you than you do! He knows how many hairs are on your head; He knows how many hairs will be on your head the day you die. He is ALL-KNOWING! He knows everything!

Romans 8:28 says, "In all things God works for the good of those who love him, who have been called according to his purpose." We are called according to His purpose! So the only stipulation is do you love Him? If you do, God will work all things for your good! It's an amazing thought! If you love God, He will work everything for your good! No exceptions!

There is no "free pass" in this life. We have a mission and we must accomplish it. If you do not fix the problem you were created to solve, it will get worse and create other problems (no wonder the world population has been growing exponentially!) So press in and find your mission!

CONSIDER:

- Find your purpose. Usually, it consists of something you are good at and love to do!

  _____

  _____

  _____

  _____

- Stop thinking of yourself as "merely human" and think of yourself as God sees you!

  _____

  _____

  _____

  _____

ACTION:

- Call out your purpose! Determine that you will fulfill God's call on your life.

  _____

  _____

  _____

  _____

  _____

  _____

  _____

  _____

  _____

  _____

- Call out the purpose in others. Sometimes people do not know how to determine their purpose and God will speak through someone else. If God speaks to you about another person's purpose . . . call it out!

  _____

  _____

  _____

  _____

  _____

  _____

  _____

  _____

  _____

  _____

Day 9

"If anyone desires to be first, he shall be last of all and servant of all."

Mark 9:35 (NKJV)

You are a servant. This is how most Christians see themselves. We are servants. When we are in the presence of others, we are to put them before ourselves and serve them!

Servanthood is always looked at negatively. Many believe that being a servant and being a slave is the same thing, but they are different. Slaves are forced into work without any guarantee of a better life or rights. Servants are usually hired hands to help whoever they were hired by. We might also call servants "maids" or "butlers." These people usually choose to work in this way, just like we need to choose to be a servant.

As a servant we are to make every effort to put others before ourselves. Jesus said that to be first we must become the servant of all. Those who serve are first in the Kingdom. Being a servant brings us closer to Jesus; after all He came to serve as well. Even though He is the King and the Ruler of all, He came to earth to serve.

If we are to become like Jesus, the best way to accomplish it is to serve everyone that comes to us. After all, no one that came to Jesus was turned away. Everyone that asked for a miracle received one!

CONSIDER:

- How do you serve those around you?

  _____

  _____

  _____

  _____

- Do you serve everyone that asks you for help?

  _____

  _____

  _____

  _____

ACTION:

- Over the next week serve others every opportunity you can.

_____

_____

_____

_____

_____

_____

_____

_____

_____

_____

_____

_____

_____

_____

_____

_____

_____

_____

_____

_____

_____

_____

_____

_____

_____

_____

Day 10

"He has made us kings and priests
to his God and Father."

Revelation 1:5-6 (NKJV)

Next on the list of who we are . . . Royalty! We are royalty! Most of us here in the United States do not understand royalty like other countries, but we have heard so many stories throughout our life to understand the basics.

Being royalty means something. It means that you are in charge or in control of something or someone. Being royalty comes with responsibility. On earth, we are in control of everything this planet has to offer. Genesis 1:28 (NCV) says "God blessed them and said, 'Have many children and grow in number. Fill the earth and be its master. Rule over the fish in the sea and over the birds in the sky and over every living thing that moves on the earth.'" God called us to be in control of all that He created. We are royalty over everything in creation.

The Bible is full of these examples. We are told that we will receive crowns in Heaven that we will throw at Jesus' feet. One of these is the Crown of Life that is given to those who have persevered under trial. We also read about the parable of the minas. In this parable, one of the servants was given ten minas and eventually he earned ten more. When his master returned he rewarded this servant saying "Well done, my good servant! Because you have been trustworthy in a very small matter, take charge of ten cities." That is supernatural increase! This servant just got promoted from the lowest class in society (servant) to the highest class (ruler). This should sound very familiar to most of us because this is exactly what happened to us when we got saved! We changed from servants to royalty!

Let's look at this thought another way. We have all heard that God is the "King of kings." That places the "King" part on God, but who are the "kings?" We are! He is the King of us, the King of Kings!

So what does this mean for us? It means that we have power and authority over creation. It is perfectly "legal" for us to command the swarm of termites, ants, spiders or other "pests" to leave our house or for the river to part so you can walk through on dry ground. We can command the mountains to fall into the sea and they must move! In fact, Mark 11:23 says "Truly I tell you, if anyone says to this mountain, 'Go, throw yourself into the sea,' and does not doubt in their heart but believes that what they say will happen, it will be done for them." We are the kings and queens of creation!

CONSIDER:

- What does being royalty mean to you?

  _____

  _____

  _____

  _____

- Do you recognize the fact that you are supposed to rule over all of creation?

  _____

  _____

  _____

  _____

- What kinds of supernatural increase have you experienced since your salvation?

  _____

  _____

  _____

  _____

ACTION:

- Take your rightful place as ruler of creation today. Take charge in the Spirit. Command animals, water and mountains to be moved! Remember you are a king or queen!

- Make decisions today with the understanding that you have a responsibility to act like royalty.

Day 11

"Love the LORD your God and serve Him
with all your heart and with all your soul"

Deuteronomy 11:13

You are a lover! As the bride of Christ we need to be passionate lovers of God. This is far more than just being a casual acquaintance that meets with God every Sunday morning and occasional Wednesday nights. A lover is someone that cannot live without the other person. As a lover of God it is our privilege to seek Him in everything.

If we remember the days when we were dating; we would remember that we called and visited our significant other every day. In fact, there were probably times when we would come home from their house and immediately call them, just to talk to them again. This is a good picture of what communication should be between God and us. We come home from church on Sunday and can't wait to talk to Him again.

Our relationship is also like our marriages as well. It is the passion and intimacy of marriage that God is looking for. When you are married, your spouse knows everything about you. They even begin finishing your sentences because they know what you are thinking. Again, this is what our relationship with God should be. We should be so in tune with Him that when He speaks to us, we can finish His sentences.

I heard a great quote that illustrates this point very well. It says, "Before God, I'm an intimate. Before people, I'm a servant. Before the powers of hell, I'm a ruler, with no tolerance for their influence." The trick is knowing when to be each one.

CONSIDER:

- What kind of lover are you?

  _____
  _____
  _____
  _____

- What can you do to make yourself into a better lover?

  _____
  _____
  _____
  _____

ACTION:

- Devote yourself to being a more passionate and intimate lover of God.

_____

Day 12

"He has made us kings and priests to his God and Father."

Revelation 1:5-6 (NKJV)

Today we are looking at the idea of being priests (or priestesses as the case may be). This seems to be a bland identity, but it is a major part of our history. In ancient times only one of the twelve tribes of Israel had the privilege for being known as priests, the tribe of Levi. Priests were usually one of few people that were literate and read from the Torah scrolls (Genesis to Deuteronomy). They were also the only people that were able to enter the Tabernacle of Moses and later the Temple of Solomon. The High priest was the only person that was able to enter the Most Holy Place and put the sacrificial blood on the Ark of the Covenant, which is God's footstool according to First Chronicles 28:2 and he was only allowed in the Most Holy Place once a year!

But then came David. David was the first King *and* Priest. He was anointed as king of Israel while Saul was still king and eventually took the throne after Saul's death. He was also often found in front of the Ark of the Covenant dancing and praising God as a priest.

One of David's biggest legacies is that he yearned for the heart of God. He wanted to do whatever God wanted and he understood that it was far more than following a set of rules and regulations that the priests had been proclaiming for generations.

Because of his insight, David set up a worship time in front of the Ark of the Covenant that NEVER ended during his lifetime. He realized that God deserved praise and that He longed for the love of His children. So David gave it to Him, every second of every day!

The next King and Priest is Jesus. He is our High Priest who went into the heavenly Most Holy Place and put His own sacrificial blood on the Ark of the Covenant that is in Heaven. And I'm sure we all know that when He returns, He is coming back to rule and reign as king!

So what does that say about us? It says that David was a man before his time. He got access into the new covenant and was able to be a king and priest in the times when they were supposed to be separated. It says that Jesus is the ultimate King and Priest that took what David did to the next level. And, of course, we are supposed to follow Jesus' model. If Jesus called us kings and priests, that is what we are! Live your life as the priest (or priestess) that you are!

CONSIDER:

- When you think of the word "Priest" what do you think of?

  _____

  _____

  _____

  _____

- What is the role of the priest in the New Testament church?

  _____

  _____

  _____

  _____

- As a priest, are you fulfilling the "duties" of the priest?

  _____

  _____

  _____

  _____

ACTION:

- Make a list of things that you believe are the responsibilities of a New Testament priest (Acts and 1 and 2 Timothy would be a good place to start). Then work hard to accomplish them!

_____

_____

_____

_____

_____

_____

_____

_____

_____

_____

_____

_____

_____

_____

_____

_____

_____

_____

_____

_____

_____

_____

_____

_____

_____

_____

_____

_____

_____

_____

_____

_____

Day 13

"Now to each one the manifestation of the Spirit is given for the common good."

1 Corinthians 12:7

Every follower of Jesus is highly gifted. 1 Corinthians 12 is all about the gifts of the Holy Spirit. You are gifted to promote the common good. If your gifts are not helping the common good, you will need to redirect them.

Many gifts of the Spirit are mentioned throughout the Bible, but 1 Corinthians 12 is one of the largest collections of such a list. Over the next few days we will dig deeper into each gift. It is VERY important that you learn to recognize these gifts in others and in yourself. Every believer has access to every gift of the Spirit. Some gifts are very prevalent while others are hidden away and need lured out. Regardless, we all have the ability to perform these gifts through the Spirit. The gifts of the Spirit include:

- Message of Wisdom
- Message of Knowledge
- Faith
- Gifts of Healing
- Miraculous Powers
- Prophecy
- Distinguishing between Spirits
- Speaking in Tongues
- Interpretation of Tongues

These gifts are so important to the body of Christ. We must use these gifts to fulfill our purpose for living. Without them we tend to fall into a religious mindset that promotes religious form without power. We cannot lose focus on the fact that our bodies are not just the home for our soul, but also for the Holy Spirit. He lives in us too and will give us amazing gifts to show others Who else is living inside us.

The critical concept here is realizing that you are more than just a human body. You have capabilities that would not exist if it were not for the Spirit's existence in you. Your gifts are given to you by the Spirit and you must use them. If you do not use your gifts, the world will never get to see that combination of your personality mixed with your gifts that God created.

CONSIDER:

- Think through the list of gifts, which do you think you have? Which gifts would others say you have?

  _____

  _____

  _____

  _____

- Think of how you can use those gifts in your daily life.

  _____

  _____

  _____

  _____

ACTION:

- Search the internet for a "Spiritual Gifts Test" and take it.

  _____

  _____

  _____

  _____

- Give the same test to someone else that is close to you and have them take it for you.

  _____

  _____

  _____

  _____

- Compare the results!

  _____

  _____

  _____

  _____

Day 14

"To one there is given through the Spirit a message of wisdom, to another a message of knowledge by means of the same Spirit, to another faith by the same Spirit"

1 Corinthians 12:8-9

The first three gifts of the Spirit that we will mention are the gifts of wisdom, knowledge and faith.

One of the biggest misconceptions about these gifts is that knowledge and wisdom are the same gift. This is not true. Knowledge and wisdom are similar, but they are still different. The knowledge gift refers to the retaining and recalling of information. Basic knowledge keeps you from ignorance. Wisdom is different because it is more theoretical. Wisdom is knowing, understanding *and* applying the information into life.

The Spirit's gifts of knowledge and wisdom are far beyond human capability. The gift of knowledge is having information about a topic that, by your own ability you would normally know nothing about. For example, my dad is a mechanic and his knowledge about cars is vast. In contrast, my knowledge of a vehicle's inner workings is limited to knowing that if you turn the key, the car should work. If I were to sit down with my dad and have a conversation with him about the intricate details of the operation of a car that would be a gift of knowledge. It would be information that the Spirit spoke through me that I never knew on my own. The gift of wisdom is similar. It is supernaturally being able to make the right decisions about a problem. The story in 1 Kings 3 about the two women that each claimed to be the mother of the living child is an example of God's gift of wisdom. If it was a gift of knowledge, God would've just told Solomon which woman was the mother of the living child. Instead he offered to have the child cut in half and to give each potential mother half a child. The situation was resoled when the real mother said that she would rather have the other woman take her child than for the child to die, Solomon realized that only the child's real mother would be willing to make that sacrifice. That is the gift of wisdom in action!

The next gift we will delve into is the gift of faith. As Christians, we all have a measure of faith. It is because of faith that we came to Christ in the first place. Ephesians 2:8 says that, "For it is by grace you have been saved, through faith—and this is not from yourselves, it is the gift of God." Our salvation is because of faith!

A gift of faith is a supernatural increase of faith in us. It is when the Spirit implants so much faith in us that we cannot help but believe in the impossible!

To put it in perspective, let's say you come across an accident that has severe injuries or even a death. A gift of faith operating in you would be if you suddenly have the realization that the injured would be miraculously healed and the dead raised! What an amazing gift! Praise God that we see this gift of faith operating in the world today!

Whether you have a gift of knowledge, wisdom or faith, they are to be used for the common good!

CONSIDER:

- Do you recognize any of these gifts in yourself or others?

  _____

  _____

  _____

  _____

- How can you cultivate these gifts within yourself and those around you?

  _____

  _____

  _____

  _____

ACTION:

- We all possess each gift of the Spirit, we are given the gifts in measure as the Spirit determines. Call out and cultivate these gifts within yourself and others!

_____

_____

_____

_____

_____

_____

_____

_____

_____

_____

_____

_____

_____

_____

_____

_____

_____

_____

_____

_____

_____

_____

_____

_____

_____

_____

Day 15

" . . . to another gifts of healing by that
one Spirit, to another miraculous powers,
to another prophecy"

1 Corinthians 12:9-10

The next three gifts we will walk through are the gifts of healings, miracles and prophecy.

The gift of healing is pretty self explanatory. It is a gift from the Spirit that enables you to heal all kinds of sicknesses and diseases. Healings were purchased at Calvary. Isaiah 53:5 says "by his wounds we are healed." The gift of healing is given to believers so that they are supernaturally able to heal! These people walk into hospitals and compete against the doctors to see how many people God will heal in the waiting room before they get called in to see the doctor. Those with the gift of healing are so confident that they expect God to heal through their hands and are disappointed if a miraculous healing does not occur.

The next gift is the gift of miracles. This gift can include the gift of healing, but it is not limited to it. Miracles can include everything from healing to calling down fire from Heaven! Those with the gift of miracles are in tune with what is going on in Heaven. They are able to see what God wants to happen on earth and they pull it down from Heaven.

The last gift for the day is the gift of prophesy. This gift is one that is very misunderstood. When most people hear about the gift of prophesy they immediately think about people that are able to predict the future. This is a part of prophesy, but it is far from a complete definition. Those with the gift of prophesy hear from God and then relay that information to the church. Many people go to someone with the gift of prophesy hoping that God will tell them what they are supposed to do with their life, and that is certainly possible, but God may just want to tell them how proud He is of them or how much He loves them or even to reinforce something that God had already placed on their heart.

I had an experience just like that. I went to a conference that is centered on the prophetic. I walked into a room full of people that were prophesying over others. I got excited! I had gotten so involved in reading and studying the Bible that I desperately wanted to know what God had in store for me. As they began to prophesy over me, I noticed that a lot of it was about how God loved me right where I was. I was told that I was going to do a lot in my school and that God saw me as a great father (I had two kids at the time) and was very proud of me. I walked out of the room thankful for my word from God even though it did not answer the questions that I had at the time.

The gifts of healing, miracles, and prophesy are all given by the Spirit and are to be used for the building up and good of mankind!

CONSIDER:

- Do you recognize any of these gifts in yourself or others?

  _____

  _____

  _____

  _____

- How can you cultivate these gifts within yourself and those around you?

  _____

  _____

  _____

  _____

ACTION:

- We all possess each gift of the Spirit, we are given the gifts in measure as the Spirit determines. Call out and cultivate these gifts within yourself and others!

_____

_____

_____

_____

_____

_____

_____

_____

_____

_____

_____

_____

_____

_____

_____

_____

_____

_____

_____

_____

_____

_____

_____

_____

Day 16

" . . . to another distinguishing between spirits, to another speaking in different kinds of tongues, and to still another, the interpretation of tongues."

1 Corinthians 12:10

The last three gifts of the Spirit are distinguishing between spirits, speaking in tongues and interpreting tongues. These gifts are extremely important to the church and need to be encouraged and cultivated.

Distinguishing between spirits is fairly self explanatory. It is a supernatural ability to determine what kind of spirit is on a person, movement, or idea. People that have a gift of distinguishing spirits can come near someone and be able to determine if there are good or bad spirits on them. This is really important in the beginning of a great move of God. People that can distinguish between spirits will affirm the move of God and be able to help find anyone that is trying to undermine the move of God.

The next gift is speaking in tongues. This gift is multifaceted. One form of speaking in tongues is a prayer language. This is a language that you pray to God with—a personal love language. There are times when you know you need to pray, but do not know how you should pray. When this happens, a prayer language is helpful to allow the spirit to talk for you. When you pray in your natural language (English, Spanish, etc.) you have the ability to allow your brain to influence what you are saying. If you are praying in your own prayer language, there is no way your brain can "mess anything up" because your brain cannot interpret your words. Speaking in tongues is allowing your spirit to speak directly to the Holy Spirit. The other form of speaking in tongues is done in a church setting for the edification of the church. This form of tongues is interpreted for the congregation to understand. It is a direct word from God and a form of prophecy!

The final spiritual gift is the interpretation of tongues. Obviously this gift allows the person to interpret the words that are spoken by someone that has the gift of speaking in tongues. These people have the ability to hear the tongues spoken and immediately understand what God is saying through that person. The church looks to these people for the word of the Lord.

All of these nine spiritual gifts are given to every believer. It is the responsibility of the believer and the church to cultivate these gifts and express them!

CONSIDER:

- Do you recognize any of these gifts in yourself or others?

  _____

  _____

  _____

  _____

- How can you cultivate these gifts within yourself and those around you?

  _____

  _____

  _____

  _____

ACTION:

- We all possess each gift of the Spirit, we are given the gifts in measure as the Spirit determines. Call out and cultivate these gifts within yourself and others!

_____
_____
_____
_____
_____
_____
_____
_____
_____
_____
_____
_____
_____
_____
_____
_____
_____
_____
_____
_____
_____
_____
_____
_____
_____
_____
_____
_____

Day 17

"So Christ himself gave the apostles,
the prophets, the evangelists, the pastors
and teachers, to equip his people for
works of service"

Ephesians 4:11-12

Most believers know of the Gifts of the Spirit, but are unaware that Christ also gave gifts to the church. Those that have heard this preached have usually heard it labeled as the "Five-fold Ministry." Although this is true, Ephesians clearly calls them a gift from Christ. The Gifts of Christ are Apostles, Prophets, Evangelists, Pastors and Teachers. Now some of these sound familiar to the Gifts of the Spirit and they can get confusing unless you know the difference. The Gifts of the Spirit are all given to every believer and all Christians can operate in every gift. The Gifts of Christ are given to believers that will ALWAYS operate in these offices. A great example of the difference is that all believers can prophesy because they received the Spirit's gift of prophecy. However, there is a difference between a believer who gives a prophecy once a week and someone that has Christ's prophetic gifting and literally lives, eats and breathes prophecy. There is a difference between someone that can prophesy and a prophet. I am not a prophet, because I do not have Christ's gift of prophecy, but I have prophesied over people because I am spiritually gifted to prophesy as the Spirit leads.

The first of Christ's gifts is that of an apostle. An apostle is a direct link to Heaven that hears what God is doing in the Earth and helps bring it about. An apostle may hear that God is calling for the salvation of children in India and begin to go through the process to create an orphanage, schools, churches or other things that God calls for to bring his words into a physical reality. Apostles are usually planners and organizers. They are the ones that will pray and fast for breakthrough and keep God's word as the primary objective in their life until God says otherwise.

The next of Christ's gifts is that of a prophet. As I mentioned before, there is a difference between the spiritual gift of prophecy and Christ's gift of Prophets. Prophets are another direct connection between God and the church. They are commonly seen as the mouth of God. They hear what God wants to communicate to the church and they tell the church what God is saying. Prophets have two major jobs, foretelling and forthtelling. Foretelling is what most people think of when they consider what a prophet's job is.

Foretelling is when the prophet is able to predict what is going to happen in the future. Forthtelling is less known about, but also very beneficial. Forthtelling is when the prophet encourages the church about what God is saying about them.

Apostles and Prophets are Christ's gifts that are a direct connection to God. They hear and see what God is doing in the Earth and they set their hearts in alignment with His.

CONSIDER:

- What are the differences between the Gifts of the Spirit and the Gifts of Christ?

  _____
  _____
  _____
  _____

- Do you recognize either of these gifts in yourself or others around you?

  _____
  _____
  _____
  _____

ACTION:

- Pray about what office God may be calling you into. If you feel lead into one of Christ's gifts, dive in head first! Do not let up, God has called you into something special!

_____

_____

_____

_____

_____

_____

_____

_____

_____

_____

_____

_____

_____

_____

_____

_____

_____

_____

_____

_____

_____

_____

_____

_____

_____

_____

Day 18

"So Christ himself gave the apostles,
the prophets, the evangelists, the pastors
and teachers, to equip his people for
works of service"

Ephesians 4:11-12

The other Gifts of Christ are that of the Evangelist, Pastor and Teacher.

The believers that are a part of the office of the Evangelist are those that are engrossed in bringing unbelievers into the family. They are the ones that can turn any conversation into an invitation to accept Christ into their hearts. We are all called to bring unbelievers into the knowledge of Jesus, but those that are Evangelists are more extreme. While most believers have brought 5 or 10 believers to Christ, Evangelists have brought hundreds.

The next gift is the Pastor. Pastors are equipped with extreme measures of compassion and understanding. These believers are amazing in relating with others. They are counselors and motivators. They are people-orientated and will help comfort and support anyone they come across.

The last gift of Christ is the Teacher. The teacher is exactly what it sounds like. It is someone that is supernaturally gifted at understanding the deep things of Christ. Teachers receive deep understanding through their studies and relay that revelation to other people.

Each of the Gifts of Christ are given to believers that give their life to the office that they are called to. Apostles, Prophets, Evangelists, Pastors and Teachers are all needed in each and every ministry and they all serve their purposes in God's government.

The best way to explain their roles is to see how they operate in the church. The Apostle prays for and announces when God's anointing is at hand. The Apostle would get others to recognize the anointing and jump into the act as soon as possible. For example if the anointing was for healing, the apostle may ask the congregation if anyone feels heat in their hands. If they do, they should begin ministering to the sick and injured. The Prophet prays for advanced knowledge of what God is doing and because of this information they are able to rebuke the spirits that are causing the problems. The Prophet also calls out the destinies of those standing around, especially those that the apostle may have pointed out as being anointed. The Evangelist has the ability to recognize unbelievers and lead them into salvation through casual unobtrusive conversation. The Pastor is the one with the personal touch. They know the names of everyone in the congregation and will be the first to help others when the need arises. Finally, the Teacher is the one that receives revelation from God and must relay that information to the rest of the church. They are the ones you typically see on Sunday mornings preaching from the pulpit. Having this understanding makes it much easier to see the differences in the administration of your church. Recognize and honor those that God has gifted with these gifts of Christ.

CONSIDER:

- What are the differences between the Gifts of the Spirit and the Gifts of Christ?

  _____

  _____

  _____

  _____

- Do you recognize either of these gifts in yourself or others around you?

  _____

  _____

  _____

  _____

ACTION:

- Pray about what office God may be calling you into. If you feel lead into one of Christ's gifts, dive in head first! Do not let up, God has called you into something special!

_____

_____

_____

_____

_____

_____

_____

_____

_____

_____

_____

_____

_____

_____

_____

_____

_____

_____

_____

_____

_____

_____

_____

_____

_____

_____

_____

_____

_____

Day 19

"But the fruit of the Spirit is love, joy, peace, patience, kindness, goodness, faithfulness, gentleness and self-control."

Galatians 5:22-23 (ESV)

The next part of us that we need to come to grips with is that the Holy Spirit has given us fruits of the Spirit that we need to exercise and make more prevalent in our lives. The first three that will be discussed are love, joy and peace.

Love is the first fruit of the Spirit. When someone is born again, the Holy Spirit gives them the capacity to love. Prior to their salvation, they showed some sort of strange love that probably stemmed from lust or selfishness. Love cannot exist apart from God, because God is love. This fruit of the Spirit enables us to love everyone, including the unlovely and our enemies.

The next fruit of the Spirit is joy. Joy is *extreme* happiness regardless of circumstances. It is also something that can only exist when God is present. Being joyful is mostly shown through a constant positive and easy-going attitude. Joyful people laugh a lot and sometimes it is about nothing!

Peace is usually defined as the lack of war, but I'd rather define war as the lack of peace. Peace is quiet tranquility. Peaceful people are not easily aggravated and often are very understanding about anything. They usually settle disputes and help to find common ground for everyone to enjoy.

Love, joy and peace are very important fruits of the Spirit mainly because we cannot have them apart from God. The Spirit gives them to us freely when we become saved.

CONSIDER:

- How have you shown love, joy and peace to others around you in the last week?

  _____

  _____

  _____

  _____

- How do you think your life would be now if you didn't have these fruits of the Spirit?

  _____

  _____

  _____

  _____

ACTION:

- Cultivate these fruits within yourself and show them daily!

_____

_____

_____

_____

_____

_____

_____

_____

_____

_____

_____

_____

_____

_____

- Resolve to be more loving, joyful, and peaceful.

_____

_____

_____

_____

_____

_____

_____

_____

_____

_____

_____

_____

_____

_____

Day 20

"But the fruit of the Spirit is love, joy, peace, patience, kindness, goodness, faithfulness, gentleness and self-control."

Galatians 5:22-23 (ESV)

The next three fruits of the Spirit are patience, kindness and goodness. Patience is one of those fruits that we tend to pray for a lot! I have heard many prayers for God to give them patience in a situation. I always silently chuckle to myself when I hear that because I know that they already have all that they need and they simply need to access it within themselves. Not to mention, the only way to develop patience is to be put in situations in which you need to be patient! Most people will pray for more patience and then get upset with God that they are going through a rough time in their life. Perhaps, that rough time is the answer to your previous prayer. It is a part of your life to give you more patience. People that are patient usually are not in a hurry. They may have an expectation of when something should occur, but they are more excited that it occurs than the time frame in which it occurs.

The next fruit of the Spirit is kindness. Kindness is a fruit that shows grace and mercy to those around you. Kindness shows itself through your relations with others. Kind people show their love through an action.

Goodness is very similar to kindness. Goodness is doing the right thing even if it is difficult. It is a very deep understanding that you will do what you need to do regardless of consequences because it is morally right, as defined by the spirit. The morality of the situation becomes the measure for if it is considered good or bad.

CONSIDER:

- How have you shown patience, kindness and goodness to others around you in the last week?

  _____

  _____

  _____

  _____

- How do you think your life would be now if you didn't have these fruits of the Spirit?

  _____

  _____

  _____

  _____

ACTION:

- Cultivate these fruits within yourself and show them daily!

_____
_____
_____
_____
_____
_____
_____
_____
_____
_____
_____
_____
_____
_____

- Resolve to be more patient, kind and good.

_____
_____
_____
_____
_____
_____
_____
_____
_____
_____
_____
_____
_____
_____
_____

Day 21

"But the fruit of the Spirit is love, joy, peace, patience, kindness, goodness, faithfulness, gentleness and self-control."

Galatians 5:22-23 (ESV)

The final three fruits of the Spirit are faithfulness, gentleness and self-control. Faithfulness is a matter of trust. You can have faith in many things. You have faith that a chair will remain standing and in one piece every time you attempt to sit in it. You have faith that the stove will heat only the pan you want and not cause a fire. You have faith that when you turn the key to your car, that it will start. Faith is trusting that it will do what is it supposed to do. We have faith that God will love us and look out for us.

Gentleness is how you deal with anxiety. There are some people in the world that cannot manage anxiety and will drive themselves crazy thinking about every possible bad outcome. Gentleness is remaining calm and being happy for the day that you have now and letting tomorrow deal with itself. Gentleness is a relaxing calm that washes over us when we remember that God is in control and He has our best interests at heart.

Self-control is the one fruit of the Spirit that most people "forget" about. People that possess self-control are those that hold their tongue, say only what is necessary and beneficial, and when they do talk, they say what they mean and mean what they say. They do not lose their minds, but rather are in control of it.

The fruits of the Spirit are attributes that all believers possess. As a believer, you do not need to pray for patience, love, joy, or any others on this list because they are what the Spirit brought with Him as he entered you. You have all of these qualities that you will ever need. All you have to do is allow them to become expressed in our life.

CONSIDER:

- How have you shown patience, kindness and goodness to others around you in the last week?

  _____

  _____

  _____

  _____

- How do you think your life would be now if you didn't have these fruits of the Spirit?

  _____

  _____

  _____

  _____

ACTION:

- Cultivate these fruits within yourself and show them daily!

_____

_____

_____

_____

_____

_____

_____

_____

_____

_____

_____

_____

- Resolve to be more patient, kind and good.

_____

_____

_____

_____

_____

_____

_____

_____

_____

_____

_____

_____

_____

Day 22

"But you have an anointing from the Holy One, and all of you know the truth."

1 John 2:20

You are anointed! God has anointed you to do amazing things for His kingdom!

An anointing is something that God gives you to do that may last a few minutes or for your entire life! Some people are anointed to sing a song, preach a message, prophesy, or anything else you can imagine. Some of these anointings are simply for the moment that they were received. Some speakers are anointed to preach a specific message to the church and then their anointing for preaching goes away. There is nothing wrong with this, God knows what He is doing and will anoint whoever is willing to do His work! I have been to churches that sing for over an hour before the message even begins, I love this when the worship leaders are anointed to sing the songs, but there are times when the singing is boring me to tears. The worship is not worship, it is merely singing. There are other times though when a song that will bring me to my knees in worship. Why does this happen? It is because the worship team was anointed to sing that specific song or set of songs! This type of anointing is very common. The other type of anointing is more long term. These anointings can be the gifts of Christ (apostles, prophets, evangelists, pastors and teachers) or anything else God has anointed you to do! These anointings can be lifelong missions from God. Many prophets I know are so anointed in their gift that they could give you a word down to the date and time of something happening! It is truly amazing.

You anointings are important. They are given to you as a mission from God because He knows that you are able to fulfill what He has anointed you to do!

CONSIDER:

- What have you been anointed to do in the past?

  _____

  _____

  _____

  _____

- What anointing are you operating under right now?

  _____

  _____

  _____

  _____

ACTION:

- Ask God what you are currently anointed to do or what you will soon be anointed to do and devote your life to accomplishing it.

Day 23

"He also took up the mantle of Elijah that had fallen from him, and went back and stood by the bank of the Jordan."

2 Kings 2:13 (NKJV)

We have been called to do the works of God. Now I know that this sounds familiar to an anointing, but it is different. A calling is something that you have that follows you all of your life. It is something that is your reason for living! Your calling is what keeps you alive; it is your life's goal. While anointings can come and go, a calling will not. Your calling is with you forever. Your calling is the purpose that you were placed on this earth. When God created you, He had a specific job for you to do. You were created to fix a problem that only someone with your exact qualities could fix.

There are a bunch of examples in the Bible of people that have specific callings on their lives. Abraham was to be the Father of many nations, Moses was to lead the Israelites out of Egypt, and Joshua was to lead the Israelites into the Promised Land. Nehemiah was called to rebuild the walls of Jerusalem, Elijah was called to be a prophet, and David and Solomon were called to rule over Israel. These people were all specifically placed on the Earth to fulfill their calling that God gave them. Some succeeded with few problems, others succeeded despite their struggles. Others, like Jonah, took a while to finally accept his anointing, but when he finally did, an entire city came to repentance!

Your calling is your reason for living. It is the purpose of your life. Figure out you calling and devote yourself to the fulfillment of it.

CONSIDER:

- What is your purpose?

  _____

  _____

  _____

  _____

- What has God called you to do?

  _____

  _____

  _____

  _____

- What is stopping you from accomplishing your calling?

  _____

  _____

  _____

  _____

ACTION:

- Ask God to let you know what your calling is and devote yourself to fulfilling it!

_____

_____

_____

_____

_____

_____

_____

_____

_____

_____

_____

_____

_____

_____

_____

_____

_____

_____

_____

_____

_____

_____

_____

_____

_____

_____

_____

Day 24

"The LORD bless you and keep you; the LORD make his face shine on you and be gracious to you; the LORD turn his face toward you and give you peace."

Numbers 6:24-26

As a believer, you are blessed. Blessings are benefits that come to you. Being blessed means you are highly favored.

Numbers 6:24-26 is a blessing for Israel. This is a blessing to put the name of God on a person. Blessing someone is to hope the best for someone, praising someone, thanking someone or protecting someone. In this context I like the definition "to request of God the bestowal of divine favor upon." Numbers 6:24-26 is not asking God to praise, thank or hope for the best for us. Only God is worthy of praise, God has no reason to thank us and he doesn't have to hope the best for us; he already knows what it is and could make it a reality at any time he chooses. This verse is asking God to bestow his divine and powerful favor upon us. "The Lord bless you" would become "The Lord gives you his divine and awesome favor for your life."

If God is going to bless someone in his name, there is no way that he will fail to follow through! His promises are everlasting and are unconditional! This verse's phrase "The Lord bless you" is saying that God WILL bless you and He will do so in HIS name.

Many times in our lives we say "God bless you" but rarely is it said without being proceeded by a sneeze. Asking God to bless someone is something that needs to be done over and over again daily! Asking God to have divine favor on someone else's life would cause anyone to draw nearer to Him.

CONSIDER:

- When was the last time you asked God to bless someone?

  _____

  _____

  _____

  _____

- Do you recognize the blessings that are on your life?

  _____

  _____

  _____

  _____

- How do you know that God is blessing you

  _____

  _____

  _____

  _____

ACTION:

- Create a list of blessings.

  _____

  _____

  _____

  _____

  _____

  _____

  _____

  _____

  _____

  _____

  _____

- Create a list of people that you want God to bless and ask Him
  to bless them!

  _____

  _____

  _____

  _____

  _____

  _____

  _____

  _____

  _____

  _____

  _____

  _____

  _____

Day 25

"Now if we are children, then we are heirs—heirs of God and co-heirs with Christ, if indeed we share in his sufferings in order that we may also share in his glory."

Romans 8:17

We are heirs to the throne of God. As the King, God sits on the throne of heaven and as His children; we are heirs to that throne. There is a lot more here than just a line of rulership. We are also heirs to the riches of God.

The first thing I want to do is prove that we are heirs. Simply put, we are the children of God in the same way that Jesus is God's Son. We are the brothers and sisters of Jesus and, therefore, we will share in the inheritance of the Father. Our status as sons and daughters guarantees us that right and privilege.

Being an heir includes many things. One aspect to being an heir is replacement. This includes a king or ruler being replaced by the nearest living relative. This is currently still in place in several countries, but none more famous than in England within the royal family. Now in Christ, we have a heavenly lineage in which we are in line for the throne. Another part of being an heir includes receiving the inheritance. God has built up an amazing inheritance for each and every believer that he passes on to us. This inheritance is full of the gifts of the Spirit and the gifts of Christ. It is also a right of blessing. When we became believers we became eternally blessed, there is nothing that can stop God from blessing us beyond measure. Some think about the bad things in life and ask where God's blessings were in that part of their life, but usually when they look back at it, they recognize that the experience made them who they are today.

We are co-heirs with Christ! His inheritance is the same as ours. Enjoy it!

CONSIDER:

- What is Jesus' inheritance?

  _____

  _____

  _____

  _____

- What rights and abilities does Jesus have as the Son of God?

  _____

  _____

  _____

  _____

ACTION:

- Make a list of the gifts that God has given to you as your inheritance. Cultivate them!

_____

_____

_____

_____

_____

_____

_____

_____

_____

_____

_____

_____

- Continue to look for more blessings from God. He is not done blessing you!

_____

_____

_____

_____

_____

_____

_____

_____

_____

_____

_____

_____

Day 26

"Therefore go and make disciples of all nations, baptizing them in the name of the Father and of the Son and of the Holy Spirit, and teaching them to obey everything I have commanded you. And surely I am with you always, to the very end of the age."

Matthew 28:19-20

As believers we are a voice to the nations. God has made it clear that He wants us to reach the nations for Him. In fact, the Great Commission of Matthew 28:19-20 says to "go and make disciples of all nations." It does not say to make disciples of every person. His desire is for the nations to bow to Him.

Missionaries are amazing people that do impossible jobs with less than adequate supplies or funds. There are missionaries in nearly every country across the planet. In fact, I have even heard of African missionaries being sent to the United States! These missionaries join a community and begin helping the natives in any way possible in order to better their lives and to show God's love for them. They build churches and schools; they dig wells and plant crops all to help out the community that they have grown to love. Once the community is self-sufficient, the missionary typically either returns home, or lives out the rest of their lives as an adopted member of the community. I love missionaries, but sometimes their vision is too small! God did not say to make disciples of all communities; He said NATIONS! Missionaries that stop short of the nation being won for Christ are cutting God short of what He desires and deserves. They are also not giving the nation what it desires. God is the desire of the nations (Haggai 2:7). Every nation longs for God.

The Bible also says to "Go into all the world and preach the gospel to every creature." (Mark 16:15 (NKJV)). Notice that it does not stop with humans. It does not say to preach to every human! It says CREATURE! I heard a great story about a man in Africa that was walking through the jungle and he noticed a bunch of monkeys playing in the trees. He smiled and laughed at their antics for a while and then he heard God tell him to preach to the monkeys. He was dumbfounded. Certainly God would not be telling him to preach to an animal. But as he began walking away, God spoke again. God reminded him that Mark 16:15 says to preach the gospel to every creature. So, after looking around to make sure no one else was watching, he began preaching the good news to the monkeys. He told them about God's love for them and His gift of salvation. As he was wrapping up, he wondered if he should also offer an altar call to the monkeys. A rustling noise in the trees broke his thoughts of the alter call and he saw several women coming out of the heavy brush. They heard his message to the monkeys and asked if it was available to them too. He was able to lead several of the women into God's kingdom because he followed the Lord's command to preach the gospel to every creature!

So how does this relate to you? You are a missionary. We all are! The Great Commission was not given to only the Evangelists or the Pastors; it was given to all believers! It is our job to be that voice to the nations that the good news of Christ has come to save them! Start with a community, but don't stop until the nation bows its knee to Jesus!

CONSIDER:

- As missionaries, it is our job to bring the good news to the nations. Too many people do not bring good news, but rather condemnation and embarrassment. Bring the good news to the nations and they will begin coming to you asking "What must I do to be saved?"

_____

_____

_____

_____

_____

_____

_____

_____

_____

_____

ACTION:

- Begin winning your nation for Christ! Start with your street or community, build up to your city, county, state and nation! Do not limit God on what He is able to accomplish through you!

_____

_____

_____

_____

_____

_____

_____

_____

_____

_____

_____

_____

- Preach the gospel to every creature, you never know who is listening.

_____

_____

_____

_____

_____

_____

_____

_____

_____

_____

_____

Day 27

"As they began to sing and praise,
the LORD set ambushes against the men
of Ammon and Moab and Mount Seir who
were invading Judah, and they
were defeated."

2 Chronicles 20:22

You are a weapon of God. This may be difficult to understand, but you are one of God's many weapons. You are what He wants to use to defeat Satan and his allies.

The best example of this is in 2 Chronicles. The enemies of Judah were coming on strong and the king, Jehoshaphat, proclaimed a fast for all of Judah so they could ask God what to do about the impending attack. Later, Jehoshaphat prays, "We have no power to face this vast army that is attacking us. We do not know what to do, but our eyes are on you." That is the key to victory; acknowledging that you do not know what to do, but that you will keep your eyes on God for guidance. After Jehoshaphat's prayer, the Lord spoke through a prophet that said that the battle was not for Judah, but for God. Essentially, God was saying "Don't worry about this one, I got it." So as the army of Judah approached the impending battle, Jehoshaphat decided to make a change. He appointed singers to march in front of the army to worship God as they came to the battlefield. Now I'm not much of a military strategist, but that sounds a bit odd. Not only are you putting unarmed men in the front of your army to be slaughtered first, but they are singing! If you had any advantage, it was the element of surprise, and I'm sure that was gone from the first note of the first song. Jehoshaphat really trusted in God to fulfill what He said through the prophet. So as Judah advanced, they began to sing and praise the Lord. As the worship came out, God began to set up ambushes for the invaders. He rode on the praise of His people and turned the men of Ammon, Moab and Mount Seir against each other. They slaughtered themselves! As the army of Judah approached the battlefield, all they saw were the dead bodies of their enemy.

God used the praise that they gave to Him as a weapon against their enemy. God does the same thing now as He did then. As we worship, God sets up ambushes for Satan. I imagine it this way. As we sing, God stirs with a desire to defeat Satan. God comes to Satan and says "See what my kids are saying about Me. See how much they praise Me. You are done for!" At this point I can see Him knocking Satan out with a mighty uppercut that sends him through the roof! Our praise causes God to come down and knock Satan around and then He tells us that we did a great job beating up on Satan! Imagine that every time you worship, God is getting in a few more punches and defeating the works that Satan has attempted to put in place. If this doesn't make you want to worship more, I don't know what will! Sing praise to the Lord for He will destroy the enemy on your behalf! You are His weapon! You are a mighty weapon of God!

CONSIDER:

- How do you worship? Worship is more than just singing. You can worship in prayer, fasting, going to work and loving your neighbor!

_____

_____

_____

_____

_____

_____

_____

_____

_____

ACTION:

- Make time to worship Him every day. Worship him in the car on the way to work, on the couch watching TV, or laying in bed before you fall asleep.

_____
_____
_____
_____
_____
_____
_____
_____
_____
_____
_____
_____
_____
_____
_____
_____
_____
_____
_____
_____
_____
_____
_____
_____
_____
_____
_____
_____

Day 28

"God saw all that he had made, and it was very good. And there was evening, and there was morning—the sixth day."

Genesis 1:31

I'm sure we have all heard the Creation Story of Genesis 1. On the first day He created light and He said it was good. On the second day He created sky and He said it was good. On the third day He created land, seas, and vegetation and He said it was good. On the fourth day He created the sun, moon and stars and He said they were good. On the fifth day He created creatures to fill the sea and rule the air and He said they were good too! (Genesis 1:3-23)

By now I hope you're seeing a pattern. God created something and the said it was good! He followed this pattern for five consecutive days, but He changed it on the sixth day. On day six, God created two things and made two different judgments. First, He created animals to roam the land and He said they were good (Genesis 1:24-25). Then comes the important difference, God made man in verse 27 and He said it was VERY good!

This little four letter word may not make a huge difference for most of us, but it should. Think of everything God created in those first six days that He said were good. He created light before there was a sun. He created the sky that separated waters on the earth from the waters in the atmosphere. He created the sun, moon, planets, and stars. He created the Grand Canyon, Angel Falls, the Sahara Desert and the Amazon Rainforest. He created every living thing that exists on the planet from gnats to eagles and plankton to blue whales and ants to elephants. God created them all and said they were good, but later, on the sixth day, God created man and He said it was VERY good! After everything else He created, He announced that it was only good, but man is far superior to everything else. Our creation was better than animals, fish and birds. It was better than the creation of the sun, moon, planets and stars. Our creation was better than the creation of plants, land, or seas. It was better than the creation of the sky and even better than the creation of light. How amazing is it that God created everything in the universe and said that we were His masterpiece! He had everything else to consider and He still said we were the best!

CONSIDER:

- In your opinion, what is the most beautiful plant, land animal, sea creature and bird in all of creation?

  _____

  _____

  _____

  _____

- In your opinion, what is the most beautiful "natural wonder"?

  _____

  _____

  _____

  _____

- Make a list of the top twenty things that God created.

  _____

  _____

  _____

  _____

ACTION:

- Is the creation of people tops on the lists you made? It is on the top of God's list! Let this idea penetrate your mind and see just how important and beautiful you are to God!

_____
_____
_____
_____
_____
_____
_____
_____
_____
_____
_____
_____
_____
_____
_____
_____
_____
_____
_____
_____
_____
_____
_____
_____
_____
_____
_____
_____

Day 29

"You are witnesses, and so is God, of how holy, righteous and blameless we were among you who believed."

1 Thessalonians 2:10

This time we are going to see that we are also holy! Holiness means that we are being set apart for the worship and service of God. As believers, we have been set apart to serve God. Many new believers see this as something we must do. It usually turns into a lifeless ritual, without meaning. For example, preachers often pound in their congregations' head that they are supposed to read their Bible everyday! This is a great practice and a great way to worship God and to learn more about Him. The downfall is that so many read their Bibles daily, but do not encounter the One that lives within the words. John 1:1 says "the Word was God." The words that you read are the essence of Who God is. Bible reading is not something to casually do so you can check it off your list of religious duties you did that day. It is a time to experience and worship your Creator! Serving God is not a duty; it is a privilege and an honor!

The second part of holiness is that we are set apart for worship. This part is amazing! Many people believe that worship is the part of the Sunday morning service when we sing. Worship is far more than that. Worship is everything you do in your life. You worship God with your voice, with your abilities, and with your family. But you show the world Who you worship when they see your priorities. For example, many people will walk into church 15 or 20 minutes late so that they will not have to sing, but these same people have no problem telling the preacher that they better be done the sermon by noon so they can get home in time to watch football. As I said, your priorities show the world what you worship and as Christians, we are set apart to worship God.

The other part of this issue is that much of the typical church's music is not really worship. Many songs and hymns were written to tell others about who God is. They are to be informational pieces to those that do not know Him. They have great purpose, but worship is usually not that purpose. We need to start singing songs to God instead of to each other. That is worship!

Here is an example. The following two selections are popular hymns; which sounds more like worship?

- "What a friend we have in Jesus, all our sins and griefs to bear! What a privilege to carry everything to God in prayer!" (What a Friend We Have in Jesus)
- "O Lord my God, when I in awesome wonder consider all the works Thy Hand hath made. I see the stars; I hear the mighty thunder, Thy power throughout the universe displayed."(How Great Thou Art)

Both are great songs, but I hope you can see the difference between singing about God and singing to God!

We have been set apart for the worship and service of God. So be holy! "I am the LORD your God; consecrate yourselves and be holy, because I am holy." (Leviticus 11:44)

CONSIDER:

- What is your attitude like when you are serving God? Do you consider it an honor, or just something to check off your "Religion List"?

_____

_____

_____

_____

- How do you worship?

_____

_____

_____

_____

ACTION:

- Spend time worshipping God. Sing songs to Him that tell Him what He means to you. Get creative and write a letter to God displaying how much you care about Him.

  _____

  _____

  _____

  _____

  _____

  _____

  _____

  _____

  _____

  _____

- Really check your motives about how and why you serve God. Are your motives for your own advancement, or for the Kingdom's advancement?

  _____

  _____

  _____

  _____

  _____

  _____

  _____

  _____

  _____

  _____

  _____

Day 30

"No one who is born of God will continue
to sin, because God's seed remains in them;
they cannot go on sinning, because they
have been born of God."

1 John 3:9

This next concept is very hard for most people to grasp. You are perfect. That's right, I said PERFECT! Now before you go crazy, let me explain.

I will start with God's creation, again. There was nothing that God created that was not good. Nothing he created had imperfections. In fact, God cannot create something that is imperfect. It is impossible for a mistake-free God to create something with a flaw. Solely based on that fact, you should realize that we are perfect. However, many of you are screaming at the page "But sin made us imperfect!" This is obviously true . . . sort of. When sin entered the body of the perfect humans, it corrupted them. It made the immortal bodies mortal. Sin caused us to begin to die and lose our perfection. However, Jesus came along and solved that problem once and for all. Many of us would agree that Jesus' death and resurrection paid the penalty for all of our sins. That meant that all past, present and future sins were covered under the redemptive work of Jesus. If that is true, then Christians can no longer sin. That's right, we are sinless! We are perfect!

How can I make such a bold claim? It's simple, and something you've probably heard a thousand times before. Jesus paid for all of our sins. It is impossible for you to sin in a way that has not already been remedied! Jesus died for that thing you will do 10 years from now, so that when those 10 years are up and you do it, He can look at you and say "What are you talking about? I put that thing as far as the east is from the west the moment you accepted me into your life!" It was gone before you did it!

Let's use an analogy. Let's say I am offering to pay your debts off completely. I will pay you back for every bill you have ever paid, pay off every bill you currently have and pay off every bill you get from this point on. You will never pay for anything else in life, EVER! Is there any way you can claim that you are in debt? The answer is no! It is the same with Jesus. He paid every debt, past, present and future! You can no longer do anything that puts you in debt!

Let's try another one. What is sin? Sin is anything that separates us from God. God promised that He will never leave us nor forsake us, which means that we cannot be separated from Him. Therefore, "Whoever abides in Him does not sin." (1 John 3:6 (NKJV)).

I know that this initially is a hard concept to receive. Our former religious teachings have muddied our thoughts, but search this out for yourselves from the Word. Meditate on it and ask the Holy Spirit for revelation.

CONSIDER:

- How does considering yourself perfect change the way you see yourself?

  _____

  _____

  _____

  _____

- Have you continued to beat yourself up over sins when they are already forgiven?

  _____

  _____

  _____

  _____

ACTION:

- Jesus has already forgiven you of everything you've done AND everything you will do. It is over and continuously beating yourself up over it is not helping. Forgive yourself!

_____

_____

_____

_____

_____

_____

_____

_____

_____

_____

- Research this concept yourself! Look it up, pray about it, and seek the Holy Spirit's guidance. He already sees you as perfect; ask Him to see yourself as He sees you.

_____

_____

_____

_____

_____

_____

_____

_____

_____

_____

_____

_____

Day 31

"Eye has not seen, nor ear heard,
nor have entered into the heart of man
The things which God has prepared for
those who love Him."

1 Corinthians 2:9 (NKJV)

One of the best things we can do in this life is know WHO WE ARE! We are not a lowly school teacher, a stay at home mom, or any other human-influenced description you can think of! You are a child of the God of the universe and He proved how important you are to Him. He had His Son die in your place! If it's true that the value of something is measured by what someone will pay for it, then we need to rethink what we are worth. To say that your life is meaningless is to say God's sacrifice for you was meaningless too! Your identity is made up of how God sees you and how you see yourself.

You are a royal child of God. You are a priest, a perfect and holy masterpiece, and the bride of Christ that was designed with a specific purpose, calling and anointing. You have gifts of the Spirit and gifts of Christ. You are a weapon that is full of the fruits of the Spirit. You are an heir to the throne of God, a voice to the nations, a lover and a servant.

You are more amazing than you probably give yourself credit for. God loves you with an amazing love that cannot be duplicated. Accept your identity and live for it. Cultivate your talents and gifts and dedicate your life to the advancement of His Kingdom.

CONSIDER:

- How do you define your life? Are you a mom, dad, brother, sister, CEO, teacher, mechanic, winner of a certain award, rich or poor? Do these classifications define your life?

_____

_____

_____

_____

_____

_____

_____

_____

_____

_____

ACTION:

- Compare how you define your life today with how you defined yourself back on Day 5.

_____

_____

_____

_____

_____

_____

_____

_____

_____

_____

_____

_____

_____

_____

_____

_____

_____

_____

_____

_____

_____

_____

_____

_____

_____

_____

_____

_____

_____

CONCLUSION

I hope that throughout the last 31 days you have come to the conclusion that you are far more important than you may have previously perceived. God sees you as an amazing creation that was made to love Him and destroy the works of the devil. You have power and authority. Take it, cultivate it, and flourish! God and His creation are longing for us to come to the knowledge of who we really are! Take dominion over the earth and claim your rightful place as a child of the King!